WHAT SHAPE SOUND

Also by John Phillips:

Language Is (San Francisco: Sardines Press, 2005)

WHAT SHAPE SOUND

JOHN PHILLIPS

SKYSILL PRESS

2011

SKYSILL PRESS
3 Gervase Gardens
Clifton Village
Nottingham   NG11 8LZ

skysillpressblogspot.com

ACKNOWLEDGEMENTS

Many of these poems have previously appeared in the following chapbooks: *Spell* (Kater Murr's Press), *Soundless* (Punch Press), *Path* (Longhouse), *Language* (Given), *A Small Window* (Longhouse), *Gone* (Hassle Press), *While* (Longhouse), *These* (Granite), *Instances* [with Roger Snell] (Third Ear Books), *Given* (Sava Books) and *Table Laid Bare* (Sava Books); as well as in the following magazines and broadsides: *Damn the Caesars, First Intensity, Shearsman, Noon, Hummingbird, kadar koli, Poetry Salzburg Review, effing magazine, Stroke, Bongos of the Lord, Persimmon, Litter* (online), *The Cultural Society* (online), *Asterisk, Tangram, Hassle* and *Empty Hands Broadside Series*

My thanks to those who cared to give them space — David Miller, Richard Owens, Bob Arnold, Jerry Tumlinson, Lee Chapman, Tony Frazer, Philip Rowland, Phyllis Walsh, Roger Snell, David Hadbawnik, Joe Massey, Whit Griffin, Andrew Hughes, Dr. Wolfgang Görtschacher, Scott Watson, Mary & Jim Taylor, Alan Baker, Zach Barocas, Jess Mynes, Jerry Redden, Mark Kuniya, Sam Ward — and to Clive Faust

CONTENTS

for Jasna, Eva
& Lana

One comes to
places curious
like years ago
recognizing
faces there
that never were

To say I will
say it in the words
there are
around me not
words yet sounds
to make
language out of
the much
not said
there is to say
I haven't said
nor will

How still the
wind not
in the leaves is
not moving just
now it was
fallen so that
dark between
each makes
still green
light leaves
away falling no
closer to see

What is not
heard yet
music still
a sounding
in my mind
some forgotten
thing less
remembered than
thought of the
first time

Less your face in
the morning
than the face in the
morning you
see
        thrown
cold
        water does
not make
feel
        or wet hands
dry

Thought a moment
it wasn't me
thinking
I was
thinking
this

Rock is
an instant
a flower is
rock   both
an instant
breaking
each rock
flower is
light

We talk thinking the words say
what we want the silence
to know we do not understand
ourselves to be

Going out
to see the moon
is part of seeing it

Remembering
it inside
is another

It is outside the wind I hear
in here listening to not a sound
other than what is heard
not listened to   rain can be
heard   not yet fallen   it will

What cannot be
spoken of you

must speak of
exactly how

you would speak
of what can be —

words are for
nothing else

but to say that
we fail to

The room
we are in
is not the same
room for each
of us   here

ACTUAL

At the back of
my head

some
thing crouching

I sit
down with

Words
sever
silence,

horde
violence

severe
enough

never to
re-
nounce

VOCATIVE

Leaning
in

to blind
wind

frantic
gulls

ransack
light

DIAGNOSTIC

To recognize absence
say yes
to a presence
not there yet
no where else

That one met
no longer
the same I
reaching was
gone from

The words
telling
the story

tell
a story
of words.

We like
to think
it's us

telling
the story,
that it's

our story
being told.

It isn't.

rain no

longer rain

I step

in

A SMALL WINDOW
for L. E.

The difference
    a small
window
made

       walking around
       my head

*

the wall   brings
      quiet
the sun

    shapes

*

in the wind the cold

the tree
there   opening

*

odd moment, tired

        more or less
        anyone

*

cars pass

    slow   fog burns
      up
     through

*

the opened window
a tree is

    birds   imagine

*

        gull
looking
      up to   white

horizontals

*

a tree down the road,   there

lately

*

  light
      shape of
the street

*

anywhere   it seems
we get   distance

*

leaves themselves are

   birds

*

that kind of day
   we think

 how
   or maybe it's

  the occasion

Not believing language
speaks only for itself
we insist on listening
to what the words say
we are are doing here

That there is
a way
has been said
to be known,
passed on
through those
it has failed

Look inside
each word

hope to
see an

actual thing
to touch, grasp

hold onto —

trust it is
there,

where it says
it is

Train passing
way back
down the track

passes
way ahead

before it
gets here

It is possible that thinking is
a doorway   to stand in   one
place among others   looking
at others   that may not be
possible   thinking they are

Incomprehensible —
silence to word —

breath between —

each making each
other mean

Mountains darken

brightness

falling

up

This river I
am in's
gone

ELSEWHERE
for John Martone

sun shifting

light   spaces

seeing air
slant heat

*

trees
above

birds
shine

*

this moment, those
and more

again

*

birds swirl up
        lit
  the air

    quick to

*

  leaves

   shadows
  caught

  through   slow
   sound

*

the wind lights
  up
    silence

a few spaces
    defined

*

birds disappear
   in
    light from

*

   shadows
just as soon
  to stare
     at

*

elsewhere
blossoms are
stars
these hands
older than

In front of
my head
what's missing
weighs
as if it were
      there

Years
over

looking
rail

road
tracks

talking
of

a river
the sea

If I sit
first sun

curiously
out and to

uplifted flood

how
      that time
time takes
to pass
      passes
      taking
no time
now

Swinging her
child

she swings her
self

Loss we
need to

cleave to
that which

we are
are still

to be

When the path I was on disappeared
I knew that was the path to follow

Looking back
what is seen

never is
what was seen

looking forward
to this

now we then
have to know

FOR

What I can say is
no use to
either of us

Words aren't for
what we need them
most to be

Yesterday's
hills

are not to-
day's

I walk back
on

That which
is not

even
noticed —

not till
your hands,

your head
pressed close,

grip tight
the bars.

FACT

The story is
not true

even if
what's told is.

Telling
lies.

FLIGHT

To walk under a grey sky
to walk with difficulty

and when fallen
be left there

Others pass by

go on
under a grey sky

Relentless

the body's
need to be

that which is
not meant to

last

Had I the
words for
you to
hear what I

want you to
hear me
say about
it I'd

say it,
tell it
to you,
say

here —
listen —
listen
to this

Eden was
invented

the moment
we left

DAY
for Cid Corman

Over the
    sound
invisible
    rain
heavy   quiet
    then

*

leaves

    running
      hidden
    streets
apparently
    there

*

through rain falling
        air somehow
    now
        visibly   straight

*

in the window
    there's a window
    that isn't

*

easy how
    seeing
    space is

    differently
    time

    blurred

*

rain the wind   makes
    briefly   still

*

trees are
words

slanting
through
light

*

even now is
what's happening
in this room
where you are

22.2.04

Language is
using us
for

reading it
self to
see

what we are
to say

Whatever there
is there
better say it
is real
or the night will
not end
in which you do
not find
yourself walking

What is alive
breathing
not merely
sounding
music you
listen to
that sight
takes at least
a moment to
recognize is
not there

Every time I
reach
　　　here
it is
　　further

waves
      clutch

   almost
   the shore

almost

     let go

CAGE

All sound
is music —

just as
silence is

He thinks

someone else
is thinking
him

thinking of
another

not himself

wondering who
is

SNOW FALL IN FOG

hard
to
see
either

through
both

That story you always thought
you had to tell was never yours
to know or tell   Even so
you tried to tell it just
the same   As if any story told
proved the teller true

ECHO

What we
listen to

the sea for
we are

The words want to know
what they are here for,
ask us to answer

WRITTEN

Flinch silence
back to

black
smeared with

thinking
words can't be

found for

...

Edge to
light

sliced
silent

within
thought's

fracture

...

Light
collapses,
back,

slack,

into it-
self —

stammer-
ing,

strewn

MARKINGS

scratched in
sand,

        low tide

OWN

The mirror never knows
whose face is
its

STILL

Today the sea
is alone.
   I stand,
looking at it.

It is alone.

Stillness
of air
   around
     gorse

    the hill   clear

       immediately
     dark

   *

Out
  in a
   circle round
     itself

    light lifting

 low along   over
  half lit water

*

scent of
birch
saplings
shaking
after   rising
rain

WAVES

heard
before / not
the same

each word said
meaning how
many not

              the path
cleared

river clouds
going
no
where

     twice

ocean she
brings me
her

hands too
small
for

I had no way of
knowing where I
was going to
get here

To talk think-
ing talk
helps,

questions no
answer
it is

For whose sake
each thought so
precisely given
till leaf is tree
to light of fact

On a wooden bench — in
slight rain — the child calls
back its old age

MOUNTAIN

now
old
what's
worth saying

the way to
roads don't reach

SLANT
for Joe Massey

wind
wrung
leaves un-

weighted,
unravel

...

day light clears heather
frayed fast along track
through spoil

...

in honeysuckle
light

cat piss
woven
        slantly

...

black bird thrown back a-
gainst
cold guttering
sky

...

snatch of
sun be-
neath
buzzard
hung
      light

...

wind
cracking
black branches
back,

rough gusts,

troughs, slack-
ing off

GIVEN

The place
looked for
            finds
who it was
to be
        found in —

                gull
    on the wing
of the wind

The story
not ending
or ending
beginning
another or
another not
beginning &
that story
being that
no story
happened

FIVE

My daughter
writes me
a poem —

some words
she knows
on a page,

saying what-
ever she
wants

for the sake of
hearing it
said

BLACK & WHITE
for/from Kline

Whites
turn
yellow

People
want
white

to
stay
white

for
ever
It

doesn't
bother
me

It's
still
white

compared
to
black

Something on paper
to keep alive
what is not alive
unless the marks
marked on paper
can be remembered
or forgotten
the slightest thing
there to be
referred to
does not matter
or matters little
only that the marks are
somewhere there
something on paper
to be looked at
or not

Look, the sky's still there.
It doesn't even
surprise you.   As if
one day soon you will
not look up and see
nothing looking back
at no one looking.

What I
was thinking was
thinking
            what
was I
      thinking

SENTENCE

We are someone else
ourselves
we don't know is
looking for

Outside us, words
change
the itinerary
recapture
the shape of
naming
before
another
disturbs
the sense
made

FEAST

torn
bread &
black
      olives

sickle
moon slung

The thing is
different things
mean the same

I can look at
just that much
I might want

rain on

leaf I

touch

     my fingers

with

SEEN

The morning became unusual

began to demand our attention

*

Strong sunlight,

all edge   here

*

From up where eyes
soar, slanting against wind
below

larks

descended

*

& traced at last

where spiders

had built

dew

more

tenuous

PAGES
for Ted Enslin

Although I
dare to
      think
meaning
must be
      it
remains
irrelevant

*

The faint nostalgia
perhaps
for exactly
that
that never
happened

we
lived
through

*

Even if I
understood
I would
have to
understand
I don't

*

Exact
speech

is

exact
action

*

I
had
forgotten

the way

to
look

quietly

*

As a mason,
arms folded
            a moment
gives his eye
to what is
visible
yet not
there,
        the correct
space
to see
in

*

It has become
part of
what is
being
completed
by you,
that thought
I had
before
this

*

Of all
     things
song
    how it
    falls
means
it

*

But I wonder
how alive
words
can be —

mauled so
for lies,
commerce,
trophy

*

Could mean the land
so long

the journey

a cup of water
all now

asked for

SOUNDLESS

Listening to snow
soundless at night

not quite soundless

footsteps across it
there   not there

the same

Upon my hand
silence

a weight
in it

as if an old friend
very little changed

There is
inside
thinking

another
pleasure
I know

awkwardly
I am
like

SPELL

Words make it seem
a moment more
than looking was

Peculiar grace
worth not being
silent for

In the presence of
light
    light is
dark
  a door in
the light
    inside the
light
   sharp in
the dark
     rain
     not quite
   dawning

Beneath this writing
is writing

it is written
to erase

Beneath that writing
another

written before
writing ever was